EASY READING INFORMATION SERIES

COCOA AND CHOCOLATE

Written by O. B. Gregory
Illustrated by Elsie Wrigley

© 1981 Rourke Publications
1975 O. B. Gregory

Library of Congress Cataloging in Publication Data

Gregory, O. B. (Olive Barnes), 1940-
  Cocoa and chocolate.

  (Easy reading information series)
  Summary: Describes the processes by which cocoa
and chocolate are made from cocoa beans. Includes
questions and a vocabulary list.
  1. Cocoa-Juvenile literature.   2. Chocolate—
Juvenile literature.   3. Cacao-Juvenile litera-
ture.   [1. Cocoa.   2. Chocolate.   3. Cacao]
I. Wrigley, Elsie, ill.   II. Title.   III. Series.
TP640.G73   641.3'374   81-11946
ISBN 0-86625-161-8   AACR2

ROURKE PUBLICATIONS, INC.
Windermere, Fla. 32786

COCOA AND CHOCOLATE

Cocoa is a drink.

It is made from the seeds
of the cocoa tree.

Cocoa trees need a warm climate.

Cocoa comes from warm countries
like Ghana in West Africa.

British
Isles

ATLANTIC
OCEAN

E U R O P E

A F R I C A

Ghana

Cocoa trees are grown from seed.

The seeds are planted in the ground
and they begin to grow.

When they are a few months old
the young trees are put
in a plantation.

They keep on growing
until they are about
twenty feet high.

When the trees are about five years old
the cocoa pods begin to grow.

The pods grow on the branches
and on the trunk as well.

When the pods begin to get ripe
they are cut down.

The men use long knives
to cut down the pods.

When they have done that
they split the pods open.

Inside each pod
there are about thirty seeds.

These are the cocoa beans.

When the beans are taken out
they are white and sticky.

The beans are then put in a pile
and covered with big leaves.

The leaves keep the beans warm.

After five or six days
the beans are ripe.

They have now changed color
from white to brown.

The beans are then spread out
to dry in the hot sun.

The beans are spread out to dry
for about a week.

Every day the beans are turned over
to make sure that they all dry.

At the same time
any poor beans are thrown away.

When the beans are dry
they are put into sacks.

The sacks of beans are taken to market
and sold.

Next, the sacks of beans are taken
to the nearest port.

There are no natural harbors
in Ghana.

So two harbors have been made.

The beans can now be loaded
right onto big ships.

The ships take the cocoa beans
to other countries.

When the cocoa beans reach their
destination they are taken
to the factory.

There they are roasted in big ovens.

The roasted beans are broken up
and then ground between rollers.

In the beans there is something called
cocoa butter.

If the beans are being made into cocoa,
some of the cocoa butter
is pressed out.

What is left is ground into
a very fine powder.

This powder is what we call cocoa.

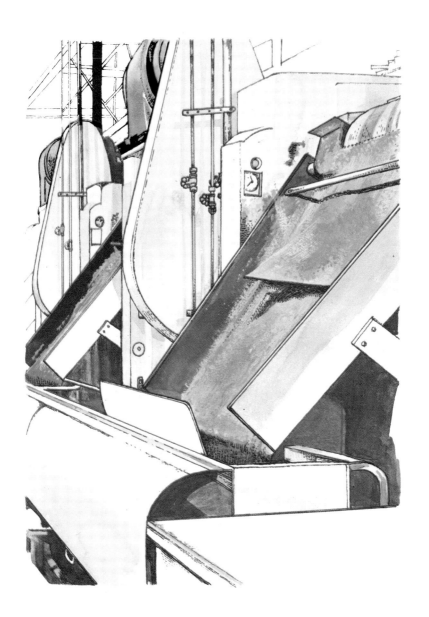

But not all cocoa beans
    are made into cocoa.

Many are made into chocolate.

If the beans are being made
    into chocolate they are roasted
    and ground just the same.

Then sugar and milk are added,
    together with more cocoa butter.

All this is mixed for a long time
    to make the chocolate smooth.

The chocolate is now made into bars.

First, it is poured into molds.

The chocolate is then cooled
　　so that it will set.

Next, the molds are emptied
　　and the chocolate is wrapped.

Sometimes fruit and nuts
　　are put in chocolate.

These are put in the chocolate
　　before it is poured into the mold.

If the chocolates are to have centers,
　　these are made first.

Then, chocolate is poured over them.

Look at the picture.

This shows chocolate doughnuts
being made.

First of all, flour, fat and sugar
are mixed together.

This is called dough.

The dough is made
into the shape of doughnuts.

After the doughnuts have been baked,
chocolate is poured over them.

The doughnuts are cooled
and put into boxes.

The boxes are taken to the stores
for us to buy.

THINGS TO WRITE

1. What is cocoa made from? (2)

2. What sort of climate do cocoa trees need? (2)

3. Name a country where cocoa beans grow? (2)

4. How are cocoa trees grown? (4)

5. How tall do cocoa trees grow? (4)

6. When do the cocoa pods begin to grow? (4)

7. Where do the cocoa pods grow? (4)

8. How do the men cut down the pods? (6)

9. How many seeds are in each pod? (6)

11. What color are the beans at
    first?   (6)

12. What color are the ripe beans?   (8)

13. Why are the beans spread out?   (8)

14. How long are the beans spread
    out?   (10)

15. Where are the beans roasted?   (14)

16. How are the beans ground?   (14)

17. Why is chocolate mixed for a
    long time?   (16)

18. Why is the chocolate cooled?   (18)

19. What are mixed together to make
    doughnuts?   (20)

20. What happens after the doughnuts
    have been baked?   (20)

VOCABULARY

CLIMATE — the general weather of a certain region. This involves air temperature, air pressure and sunshine.

PLANTATION — a very large farm with a big house and homes for the workers where a specific type of crop is grown.

PODS — a container, usually oval in shape, which holds seeds.

RIPE — when a fruit or vegetable is mature enough to be picked and eaten.

ROASTED — cooked in an oven until done.

DOUGH — when flour and water or milk are mixed together they form a pasty substance. This paste is used in the making of bread.